Grow It Yourself!

Grow Your Own
Butterfly
Farm

John Malam

www.raintreepublishers.co.uk
Visit our website to find out more information about Raintree books.

To order:
☎ Phone 0845 6044371
🖹 Fax +44 (0) 1865 312263
🖥 Email myorders@raintreepublishers.co.uk

Customers from outside the UK please telephone +44 1865 312262

Raintree is an imprint of Capstone Global Library Limited, a company incorporated in England and Wales having its registered office at 7 Pilgrim Street, London, EC4V 6LB – Registered company number: 6695582

Edited by Daniel Nunn, Rebecca Rissman, and Sian Smith
Designed by Philippa Jenkins
Picture research by Mica Brancic
Production by Victoria Fitzgerald
Originated by Capstone Global Library Ltd
Printed and bound in China by Leo Paper Products Ltd

ISBN 978 1 406 22479 5
15 14 13 12 11
10 9 8 7 6 5 4 3 2 1

British Library Cataloguing in Publication Data
Malam, John, 1957-
    Grow your own butterfly farm. -- (Grow it yourself!)
    1. Butterfly gardening--Juvenile literature.
    I. Title II. Series
    638.5'789-dc22

Acknowledgements
The author and publisher are grateful to the following for permission to reproduce copyright material: Alamy pp. 13 (© Linda Kennedy), 16 (© Brian Hoffman), 21 (© LeighSmithImages), 25 (© Blickwinkel); Photolibrary pp. 15 (Polka Dot Images), 17 (Garden Picture Library/David Askham), 19 (Garden Picture Library/James Guilliam), 28 (Garden Picture Library/Kevin Dutton); Shutterstock pp. 4 (© Studio Foxy), 5 (© Elizabeth Spencer), 6 (© Ttphoto), 7 (© Tyler Olson), 8 (© Olga Altunina), 9 (© LilKar [Jakez]), 10 (© iladm [Olga Bogatyrenko]), 11 (© Antoine Beyeler), 12 (© Inc), 14 (© Margaret M Stewart), 18 (© Trombax), 20 (© Kitigan), 22 (© Vilax), 23 (© Andrew Park), 24 (© Marek Mierzejewski), 26 bottom (© Steve Byland), 26 top (© Lori Skelton), 27 bottom (© Sari ONeal), 27 top (© James Laurie), 29 (David Dohnal).

Cover photographs of various grasses blossoming on a meadow reproduced with permission of Shutterstock (© Sever180), and a monarch butterfly on a mass of white flowers reproduced with permission of Shutterstock (© Alex James Bramwell).

Every effort has been made to contact copyright holders of material reproduced in this book. Any omissions will be rectified in subsequent printings if notice is given to the publisher.

To find out about the author, visit his website: www.johnmalam.co.uk

Some words are shown in bold, **like this**. You can find out what they mean by looking in the glossary.

Contents

Safety note:
Ask an adult to help you with
the activities in this book.

What are butterflies?

Butterflies are members of the **insect** family. They have brightly coloured wings. Butterflies are insects that can fly. They only fly in the day, not at night.

This is a brimstone butterfly.

This monarch butterfly is drinking nectar.

Butterflies feed on **nectar**, which is made by flowers. You can grow flowers that will attract butterflies. Many people enjoy watching butterflies in their garden.

What are wild flowers?

Wild flowers are flowers that grow in fields, meadows, and by the roadside. They grow wild, which means they grow where they want to. Butterflies like to feed on wild flowers.

Clover is a common wild flower.

Purple flowers attract a lot of butterflies.

There are many different wild flowers. Here are some you might know: thistle, buttercup, clover, dandelion, foxglove, poppy, and ox eye daisy.

Why do we need butterflies?

Butterflies are good **insects** to have in a garden. When they land on a flower, specks of **pollen** stick to them. They take the pollen to other flowers.

pollen

Butterflies take pollen from flower to flower.

Flowers need pollen to make **fruit** and **seeds**. Insects that move pollen from one flower to another are called **pollinators**.

What do butterflies eat?

Butterflies cannot chew food. Instead, they are drinkers. They drink water from puddles and ponds, and **nectar** from flowers. Nectar is a sugary liquid made by plants.

This butterfly is drinking water from a puddle.

proboscis

Butterflies use a feeding tube to drink through. This is called a **proboscis**. They push it into the nectar or water, then suck up the liquid.

Start your butterfly garden

You can attract butterflies by growing wild flowers. You can grow them in a garden or in a large pot. Wild flowers like to be in the sunshine, so look for a sunny place to grow them.

Find a sunny place for your flowers.

There are lots of flower seeds to choose from.

In the spring, buy a packet of wild flower **seeds**. Look for a packet that says the seeds will grow into plants that butterflies like.

Sow wild flower seeds

In early spring, clear the ground of weeds. Then, make a **seed bed** to **sow** your wild flower seeds in. Loosen the soil with a garden fork. Break up any lumps. Rake it over to make a fine, crumbly soil.

seed bed

Drag the rake across the soil.

Wild flower seeds can be tiny.

Pour a few seeds into your hand. Take little pinches of the seeds and **scatter** them across the seed bed. Use a rake to mix the seeds into the soil. Sprinkle water over the soil with a watering can.

Cats and birds – keep off!

Cats like **seed beds**. They dig up the fine soil, make a mess, and disturb the **seeds**. Birds peck up the seeds and eat them.

Cats make a mess of seed beds.

To keep cats and birds away, cover the seeds
with a cage or garden **netting**. You can take this off
when the seeds have grown into small plants.

Watering the seed bed

Keep the **seed bed** watered, especially in dry weather. Try not to let the soil dry out or the **seeds** will not grow. If it has been raining, the rain will have done the watering for you.

Sprinkle water on to the seed bed.

This tiny seedling has just been watered. ▶

After two or three weeks, look out for the tiny leaves of the first **seedlings**. It is often easier to spot them after the soil has been watered.

Add some marigolds

Butterflies like flowers that are brightly coloured and stay open all day, such as marigolds. In the spring, garden centres sell trays of baby marigold plants.

These marigold plants are in full flower.

There are a lot of marigolds in a tray.

Buy a tray of marigolds for your butterfly garden. Marigolds are shorter plants than most wild flowers, so put them in front of your wild flowers. This means you will be able to see them.

Watch your garden grow

Wild flowers grow quickly in the warm months of spring and summer. Some, such as foxgloves and ox eye daisies, will grow tall. Others are shorter, such as forget-me-knots.

Forget-me-knots are blue flowers.

flower buds

Foxgloves are tall flowers.

Look for the flower **buds**. Then watch them as they open into flowers over a day or two. Use a wild flower book to identify the flowers you have.

Butterflies have landed!

When the flowers are open, look for butterflies landing on them. Butterflies like flowers that open flat out, so they have somewhere to stand.

Forget-me-knot flowers are a good shape for butterflies to land on.

This red admiral butterfly has landed on a buddleia.

What colour flowers do the butterflies like the most? Look closely to see them drinking **nectar** through their feeding tubes.

Be a butterfly spotter

Look closely at the butterflies on the wild flowers.
Look at the colours and patterns on their wings.

This is a tortoiseshell butterfly.

This is a brimstone butterfly.

This is a purple-edged copper butterfly.

This is a speckled wood butterfly.

Are lots of different kinds of butterflies coming to the flowers, or are they all the same kind? Use a butterfly book to identify the butterflies.

Be a seed saver

Towards the end of summer, the flowers will start to die. Don't pull them up! As they **wither** and dry, the flower heads make **seeds**.

Wild flowers make seeds for next year. ▶

A poppy head holds a lot of seeds.

Shake the plants and the seeds will fall to the ground, ready to grow next year. Or you could pick off the dried flower heads. Keep them in a dry place, and you will have seeds for next year.

Glossary

buds flowers or leaves before they open

fruit the part of a plant which can often be eaten as food. Fruit contains seeds.

insect a small animal with six legs, no backbone, and a body divided into three parts

nectar a sugary liquid made by plants

netting a plastic net with holes in it

pollen tiny powdery grains made by flowers

pollinators animals, such as butterflies and bees, that move pollen from one flower to another

proboscis the feeding tube of a butterfly

scatter to spread seeds across an area by throwing them

seed the part of a plant that grows into a new plant

seed bed an area of fine soil where seeds are sown

seedling a baby plant

sow to plant a seed

wither to shrivel up

Find out more

Books to read

Ben Plants a Butterfly Garden, Kate Petty and Axel Scheffler
(Macmillan Children's Books, 2001)

Butterflies Spotter's Guide, George E. Hyde
(Usborne Publishing, 2006)

Caterpillars and Butterflies, Stephanie Turnbull
(Usborne Publishing, 2007)

Wild Flowers Spotter's Guide, Christopher Humphries
(Usborne Publishing, 2006)

Websites

www.bbc.co.uk/gardening/gardening_with_children/
plantstotry_butterfly.shtml

This website gives you information about creating a butterfly
garden.

www.leadgate-inf.durham.sch.uk/butterflygarden

Find out how a school transformed a patch of land into a
butterfly garden on this website.

Index